The "*Main*" Wife
A Memoir of Manipulation and Victory

Alex P. Midori

outskirtspress
DENVER, COLORADO

Outskirts Press, Inc.
http://www.outskirtspress.com

ISBN: 978-1-4787-3019-4

Outskirts Press and the "OP" logo are trademarks belonging to Outskirts Press, Inc.

PRINTED IN THE UNITED STATES OF AMERICA

I dedicate this book to my beautiful children.
In memory of my loving grandmother.

Foreword

You are now holding an important piece of a nurtured life. When Alex and I met, I could sense she was a writer. While you will be eager to know what happens next at the turn of a page, you also will be reflecting over your past. When she shared with me her life struggles, which ended up in this book, I was so honored to know her and needed to enlist her brave spirit. This piece of work will empower, uplift, and bring clarity to you when making decisions in life. This series of events will wake you out of your sleep. Everyone has a story to tell, and it's up to you to get it out. Fear never sleeps.

Veleta Jones
Author of *Five Layers Deep on How to Forgive*
Outskirtspress.com/fivelayersdeep

Preface

I wrote this book of my life experiences in the organization as well as my childhood to the best of my recollection. The names have been changed, including mine, in some chapters because that's the name I was going by at the time. It is my story, and I extend a sincere, heartfelt apology to anyone who was hurt or affected by any of my actions. I also view it as an opportunity to let people see who I am and not what I have been charged with or labeled as because of bad choices I made. Since my release from prison, and by way of therapy mandated by my probation, I have learned about boundaries and the responsibilities of "adults" to acknowledge their limitations within those boundaries when dealing with children. My intentions and prayer for the outcome of this book is for someone to learn from my mistakes and experiences, based on the choices I made, and maybe help someone to think twice about his or her choices before committing to them. On my journey I've learned the importance of proper choice making and how our quality of life is based upon the choices we make daily, in most cases. Every choice we make has a consequence, regardless of how uncorrupt or innocent it may be or appear to be.

Acknowledgments

Special thanks to Travis M. King, Shawn Brooks (shawnbrooksdesign.com, shawnbrooksphotograhy.com), Veleta Jones, Creflo Dollar Ministries, Alva Clemons (anaturalknockout.com), and Lynn Whittaker.

Without the grace, strength, perseverance, love, compassion, all power of my God, and the profound support of my family and the ones God brought in my path, this book would not have been possible. My life is a testimony.

Author's Note

This is a work of nonfiction. I have tried not to rewind the events in my psyche on a daily basis. Each chapter is told with sincerity and honesty. The detailed events are not only going to leave you on the edge of your seat but will leave you making a promise to yourself to never end up in the situations that I have.

In life, when we make choices, we are almost certain it's not going to affect things and people around us because they seem right to us. This book is laid out in the order of a series of events as they happened. While my life is still being shaped, the importance of getting my story out could not wait another second.

Chapter 1

The Arrest

May 8, 2002, the day that gave me freedom

For six weeks I had been on a cleansing fast. This was the last day of the fast and the first stage of my healing. As a Muslim, I fasted a lot because it was one of the five pillars of faith, and it was said to feed the spirit and make one more in tune with the spiritual realm, which is the main reason I would do it. This fast was not only for my spiritual being but also for my physical well-being. In 1999 I was diagnosed with the chronic disease multiple sclerosis and told very carelessly by the physician that I would have to inject myself every other day with medication, the side effects of which would make me feel like I had the flu for the rest of my life. Upon being told that disturbing news, my reaction was "What's the point of taking the medication if it can't cure me?" The doctor said it would slow up the progression of the disease. Now, my mother's sister died from MS, and although I was young, I remember watching the disease slowly but surely debilitate her, from being what appeared to be a healthy, beautiful Jamaican nurse who one day out of the blue (looked like to me) started walking with a cane and then crutches and finally ended up in a wheelchair as the disease consumed her until she eventually died.

I was a vegetarian and believed there had to be some

natural remedy, even though they told me there was no cure. With this belief and my faith in the Most High, I refused to take the medication and began to intensely research the disease and the proper diet I needed to be on to survive. During this fast I had been doing a lot of praying and soul searching. I was praying for deliverance from the mental prison I was in. I felt trapped mentally and spiritually stagnant, just tired of the polygamous lifestyle, I guess. I was feeling like something was happening within me, but I couldn't tell exactly what it was.

Marcus, my common-law husband of fifteen years as well as a polygamist, and I had not been around each other for several days. I needed to focus on me for a change. See, Marcus was a self-proclaimed embodiment of the angel Michael, according to his doctrine, and I believed him and treated him as such, like royalty. On this bright and sunny eighth day of May 2002, as I walked to the office (a two-story building the brothers had built for Marcus to run his businesses from) I saw Marcus. We smiled and greeted each other. I was actually happy to see him and got a warm feeling inside like old times. I guess absence does make the heart grow fonder. He asked me if I wanted to go for a ride with him. "Sure," I replied. I hadn't been out in weeks. (Let me explain, the women in the organization did not leave the community unless escorted and/or permitted.) I ran to the car without my pocketbook, I was so excited. I usually take my trusty pocketbook everywhere I go, especially when I'm with Marcus. It's not really the pocketbook that I had trust in but the .357 Magnum I carried in it. See,

Marcus believed he had enemies because of his controversial Islamic doctrine and that one day these enemies would make an attempt on his life.

Two other girls who worked in the office, Louise and Eunice, went along with us. Louise was kind of tomboyish, tall and slender, an attractive girl. Louise drove and Marcus sat in the passenger's seat while the other girl, Eunice, and I sat in the back. We went to an arts and crafts store located near Walmart in Milledgeville, Georgia, to get supplies to make some costumes for a parade we were intending to participate in. They didn't have what we were looking for, so we left, got in the Navigator, and before we could fasten our seat belts, I heard a male voice shout, "Put your hands up!" I looked up and the car was surrounded by some white men in plain clothes with rifles or AK-47s—I don't know what they were; all I know is that they were big and pointed at us. I thought to myself, "Oh my God, we're being hijacked and they're going to kill us." Then I thought this had to be a practical joke or something. I couldn't believe this was really happening in broad daylight. Were we about to die? I thought to myself in disbelief. Then again I heard "Put your hands up!" I guess we all were stunned because no one moved. Then *crash*! The window was broken in the front on the passenger side, and for the last time I heard "Put your hands up!"

Louise screamed and everyone's hands went up. We were told to step outside the vehicle, and once we did they told us to lie on the ground. I put my hands down first and kind of held myself up off the ground. I must say, even with feeling my life was on the line, I instinctively did not want to lay flat on the filthy ground. Then some boots stepped in front of me, and a male voice asked me if I was Candace Jenkins. I replied yes, and he put his boot on my back and forced me face-first down to the ground and yelled, "Got Candace Jenkins here." I couldn't help but think, "Oh my God, what are they going to do?" I was scared, but I felt numb at the same time. What was happening? By this time I assumed we weren't being robbed when a female agent approached me and took me to an unmarked vehicle. She spoke very gently and asked me if I was all right. I just stared at her because I didn't trust her or anyone else for that matter. Marcus made me feel that way, like I shouldn't trust anyone because he didn't trust anyone. Apparently, Marcus told them about my MS because she was asking me questions about my medication. I still refused to talk to her.

Louise and Eunice were not arrested, and they were escorted home. Marcus was put in an unmarked vehicle that drove off. I didn't like that; I didn't want us to be separated, but I knew if they were taking us to jail, we weren't going together. One tear rolled down my cheek as I watched him go by. That was the only emotion I showed during the whole ordeal. I felt numb and disassociated as though I was watching the whole thing from afar. Then a sudden calmness came over me and a voice from within said, "Don't worry, everything is going to be OK." I felt confident and trusted in this voice.

THE MAIN WIFE

We were taken to the federal courthouse in Macon, processed, and placed in separate holding cells. I worried about Marcus the whole time because of his health and age. He's twenty-five years older than me and had developed a chronic illness called angioedema. This illness would cause him to have an allergic reaction to stress, I reckon because that was the main thing that was consistent in his life. I kept thinking this would all be over soon and someone would come and have us released, but it didn't happen. I know now I was living in a nightmare.

Chapter 2
Unconditional Love

A little something about my family and childhood

I remember my grandmother waking up at four o'clock every morning to pray. She would go in the bathroom, close the door, and get on her knees and pray. Once she was dressed, she would go in the kitchen, put on some grits to cook, and burn frankincense (to ward off evil spirits, I guess) while she read her Bible and Daily Word devotional. This was her daily ritual for as long as I can remember, and there was something about it that I liked. I never really saw Grandma mad or raise her voice or worry and complain, unless you didn't want to go to church! No matter who it was, she would always say the same thing—"You don't want to hear the word of *God?*"—in a tone of disbelief. Grandma went to church every…single…Sunday, rain, snow, sleet, or sunshine. And guess who she had with her every…single… Sunday? Me! I'll never forget that church, a small modest church in the Bronx with about eight members (that's including the choir). The pastor was a good and sincere man, mild mannered and soft spoken, so much so that everyone (except Grandma) would fall asleep during the service unless we had a guest speaker who knew how to keep the church awake. Grandma was always the same although sometimes I could tell Grandpa got on her nerves—especially if he didn't want to go to church because the weather was bad or something—but even that was seldom. She was very giving and compassionate even though she lived on a fixed income, which was a small Social Security check each month. She always had money to spare for anyone who needed it, and I do mean anyone. At some time or another, everyone would need to borrow a few dollars from Grandma, from her sons to friends and people in the building she barely knew. Once, my father had to get on her for lending money to a woman who lived in the building and was obviously hooked on drugs, but Grandma would say, "She has children, and they need clothes and food. That's why I give to her." I noticed these things about Grandma while I was growing up: her faithfulness, generous nature, compassion, and pure love for people. I said I wanted what Grandma had when I grew up. God was the focal point in her life, and things always seemed to work out no matter how bad it appeared to be.

Grandma was an only child, and she would always tell me when she was a little girl, she would pray that God would bless her with more than one child "when she grew up to be a big lady." Well, he blessed her with five boys that she ended up raising as a single mother with the help of Aunt Bessie, a woman who was a close friend of the family from Savannah, Georgia, where my grandmother was born. Aunt Bessie played the role of disciplinarian to help Grandma with the boys because she wouldn't harm a fly. My father said he never heard his mother complain about raising them alone; she was just happy to have her prayer answered with more than one child, and they were her life. She eventually remarried, and shortly after that her youngest son died at the age of twenty-five from a heart attack.

Grandma basically raised me because she would babysit while my parents were working. When I was around nine or ten, her husband died from a stroke after twenty-five years of marriage. I couldn't stand to see her sleep alone after sleeping next to someone all those years. I asked my father if I could stay with her, and he said yes. My younger cousin and I would alternate staying with her; my cousin would stay on the weekends while I stayed during the week. This went on for a few years until my grandmother died peacefully in her sleep at the ripe old age of eighty.

The three greatest loves of my life, before my three children were born, were my faith-filled grandmother who had the greatest influence on my spirituality; my beautiful, ambitious and strong mother who taught me that God was in *me*, not in the sky or in a building called the church; and last, but definitely not least, my loving and dedicated father who taught me that God was in nature.

Let's talk about my dad because he is a very special man. I am his only child, and he told me he never really wanted any children; in fact, when my mom got pregnant, he told her that he didn't want a child, but my mother replied with authority, "I'm having this baby!" So I guess that makes me an "oops baby." Huh, that's funny to me. From the stories my parents have told me, ironically it seems as though I stole his heart from the womb. He told me when my mother was pregnant he had all the weird cravings like sauerkraut and neck bones. That's not even a black dish; it's German (go figure), according to my father. Well, he worked in a firehouse, where the men cooked for themselves and there were different nationalities working there, so that's probably where he got it from. Then, he said when I was born he would come to the hospital and just stare at me for as long as he was allowed to visit. The nurses would say, "Aw, he's such a proud and dedicated father." However, it was quite the contrary. He said I was a petite six pounds fifteen ounces, pale, and scaly with hazel eyes, and he kept staring at me because he was thinking, "They must have made a mistake. This can't be my baby; one of those cute, plump, caramel babies must be mine." Well, they didn't make a mistake, and he was stuck with me, but as I started changing, he fell in love with me even more and became my slave (giggle), waking up all hours of the night to feed me and change my diaper. He said he would take me for walks to the park in my stroller, and when I got older, he would take me to the firehouse with him. Did I mention he's a proud retiree after twenty-two years as a New York firefighter?

I was a "daddy's girl" since I was his only child, and he took me everywhere with him—to movies, plays, Broadway shows, nice restaurants, swimming, ice skating, Bear Mountain Park—everywhere except Disney World. I was obsessed with Mickey Mouse and Donald Duck because my father and uncle would call me when they were at work and talk like they were Mickey and Donald. For years I thought I was really talking to them, and Daddy would

promise me every summer that he would take me next summer to meet them in person. Negative, it never happened,
but I was still crazy about my daddy. No matter what I
was doing—I could be a mile away from him—as soon as
I would spot him, I would yell out with pure excitement
and joy, "Daaaaddyyyy!" and break into a sprint toward
him and then jump into his open arms. After a while, if
I was outside playing and I saw my father, my friends and
all the kids on my block started running with me, yelling
"Daaaaddyyyy!" Lucky for him they didn't all try to jump
into his arms too (snickering to myself). Those were the
good ole days when life was so simple.

Each one of these loves is unconditional, and each one
of their beliefs played a significant role in molding my character. I feel very fortunate to have so much love in my life.
Unfortunately, my parents got divorced when I was four.
I remember the good and the bad of their relationship. I
recall waking up one Christmas Eve to the sounds of my
parents putting gifts under the tree. My half-sister and I
shared a room, and we both heard the noise but pretended
to be asleep so we wouldn't interrupt "Santa." My sister is
eight years older than me so she probably knew it wasn't
Santa, but she went along with it so not to mess it up for
me. I don't think we slept a wink that night because we
couldn't wait to get up and see what we got. As soon as we
saw daybreak, we jumped out of bed and raced to the living room to rip open every gift we saw our name on. That
was a good memory. But I also remember them kidnapping
me from each other after they got divorced. I shouldn't

even use the term "kidnapping"; it sounds so illegal. I'll just say they would take me with them for a visit without informing the other one. One day they both came to my elementary school, SPS 131 in the South Bronx, to get me at the same time. What a coincidence. The school called me to the office, and to my surprise, when I got there both my mother and father were there. My mom was in tears. I didn't know what was going on; all I knew was that I was embarrassed this was happening in front of my teachers. I don't remember how it ended; I just remember hearing a teacher say the only reason they didn't fail me was because they felt sorry for my situation. I was caught in the middle of my parents' feud, which was causing me to miss classes, but fortunately I was a bright student and didn't give the teachers any problems.

A lot was going on with my mother at this time. She was a very proud and ambitious young woman. Five foot nine, forty-four double D, with big, gorgeous legs as my father would say. At the age of thirty-two, she owned a three-family house and a beauty shop in the Bronx. I remember her telling me that she had always liked doing hair, and when she was a little girl, she would take a fork and wrap grass strands around it like she was curling hair on a curling iron. What an imagination. My mother was born in Jamaica and came to America when she was nineteen. Then she worked her way through beauty school and took a nursing course to become a home attendant. She was a success story.

When I was around nine, on the weekends my mom would invite a few of her friends and customers from her beauty shop to the house for readings. One day, I over-heard my mother discussing one of her readings with her sister Pinky. My mom said the reading lady told her that she was going to meet a bald man who was handy and loved fried chicken. Our boiler needed to be repaired, and the lady giving the readings told my mom she knew someone who could fix it for her. The next day a man knocked at the door and said he was there to fix the boiler. While in conversation with my mother, he asked if she did men's hair. My mother replied in a strong Jamaican accent, "I can. Why, do you want something done to yours?" "Yes I do," he said. "Can you fix this toupee?" "Of course, mon," she replied. A couple of days later he came to the beauty shop to get his toupee done, and while in conversation with my mom, he mentioned that he loved fried chicken. Then it dawned on my mother that this was the man that the read-ing lady told her about. My mom seemed kind of excited, probably looking forward to whatever else the reading lady had predicted. As time went by, I found out the handy-man's name was Alvin. I noticed Alvin spending more and more time with my mom at the beauty shop as well as the house. He got so comfortable with my mom that he would take money "tips" out of her pockets, like it was his money, and Mommy wouldn't say or do anything. I found that to be kinda strange and unlike her.

We resided in a three-bedroom, one-bath apartment on the top floor of the house. One of my mother's sisters and a friend lived with us, and over some time Alvin started com-ing around more frequently. From my perspective it looked like Alvin was gradually clearing out the house because one by one they left for good, including my sixteen-year-old sister, until it was just my mother and I left in the house. My mother started acting strange. For example, one day she walked out in front of the house and just started crying and screaming at the top of her lungs. I was so afraid for her that I started crying too. I didn't know why she was acting like that. The tenant who lived on the first floor of the house came out to console her and calm her down. I don't remember what happened after that.

I remember my father coming to the house one afternoon asking me why I wasn't at school. He was there to take me to lunch. My mother didn't wake me up for school that morning, so my father came to the house to see what was going on. Shortly after my father got to the house, my mother came to check on me, I assume, and she told me she went to the bank and only had thirty-five dollars left in her account. She was upset. I could hear in her voice that she was crying. I don't know how much she had had in the account, but I know she worked her ass off for it. I told her that daddy was with me, so she asked to speak with him. After they spoke, my father told me to get some clothes because my mother asked him to take me with him.

Apparently Alvin had access to my mother's bank account and took all but thirty-five dollars of her money. This was the beginning of her nervous breakdown, and she was eventually diagnosed as bipolar, the beginning of thirty years in and out of mental institutions, being homeless, and everything else it seems but hopeless. She never lost hope. One day I asked her, through all of the trials and tribulations she endured in her life, did she ever contemplate suicide? She said no because she always hoped to get her family back together.

Chapter 3
High School (the good ole days)

1983-1987

I call the eighties the good ole days because life was basically carefree in those adolescent years. I went to A. Phillip Randolph Campus High School in Manhattan, which was located on the campus of City College, and considered to be a pretty decent school. It wasn't the best, but you had to have at least an 80 percent average to get in the school. The building was originally the old music and arts school, which moved farther downtown and combined with The Julliard School of Performing Arts. I remember on my first day being a little nervous about going to high school. My dad drove me to school the first couple of days, but I had to start taking the train by myself. I didn't know anyone there because none of my classmates from junior high school went to that school, but I was used to being alone, being an only child kind of. In one of my classes there were two girls, Michelle and Crystal, who seemed friendly because they would smile at me even though they were juniors. You know, some juniors won't associate with freshmen, but they were nice.

One day there was a flyer put up in the halls about auditions for the Miss Campus Contest, which the school was putting on for the first time. While we were sitting in the classroom waiting for class to begin, Michelle and Chrystal were talking about the contest. Michelle asked me if I saw the flyer, and I responded yes. "So you should audition. You are pretty enough to win," Michelle suggested. I replied, "Thank you, but I don't think so, and don't you have to know how to do something to audition?" "Yes, I'm sure there is something that you can do," Michelle responded with a strong sense of confidence and encouragement. "I don't play an instrument or anything, so what am I going to do, recite a poem (borrring)?" Then I thought about it. "Oh yeah (a light bulb clicked on in my head), you're right. I like to sing, so maybe I could do that." How could I forget that I listened and sang along to music every day when I got home from school and finished my homework? That was my favorite pastime. I just wasn't sure if I could sing in front of a bunch of people and if it would sound good enough. The only singing I'd ever done was when I was a little girl around four or five in the choir at church and nobody could really sing. The choir was composed of the pastor's two kids, a girl seventeen and a boy nineteen, and one of the two deacons who had about six kids (teenagers as well), so that made a choir of nine. One day the deacon and the pastor fell out, and the deacon and his family left the church, so that left three in the choir.

Well, back to the talent show. Once I decided I was going to audition I wasn't worried about it. I chose a song I felt I could sing, Stevie Wonder's "Power Flower," for the audition, and then it was popping from that point on. I love Stevie Wonder, so I chose a simple song of his that I knew all the words to and practiced it because I had to sing it a cappella; I couldn't find the karaoke version. A few days or so later I went to the audition and the judges liked me, so I made it into the contest. We had to model an outfit, so I got a black handkerchief-cut dress, very feminine and pretty, with a pair of black sling-back heels. There was a gentleman there from Class magazine who was behind the stage, and he kept complimenting me and giving me little pointers on how to walk and stuff like that. It was scary and fun at the same time because I had never done any of it before. Then it was my turn to enter the stage. I walked out sideways with my back to the audience taking each step carefully and deliberately, and when I got to the marker, I stopped and slowly turned around (the classic model turn) and then walked on. Oh, they loved it because it was unexpected. It was my turn to perform, and I was singing Gladys Knight's "You're Number One in My Book." As soon as I opened my mouth, people started cheering for me because a lot of people liked that song. There was a place in the song where everyone got quiet to see if I could hold the note or not, and I did it, so the crowd went wild. That was the best feeling ever. Then I had to answer some questions; the first was "If you had three wishes, what would they be and why?" I don't remember my answer, but this guy yelled out, "Scudder! Scudder! Scudder!" and everybody burst out laughing. See, everyone knew Scudder because he was a super senior (twenty in the twelfth grade). However, I didn't win. I came in first runner-up, and I think it was because I was a freshman, because based on the audience reactions to my performances, I should have won. The girl who won was a senior, just FYI. All that experience did was stir up something within me because next I wanted to perform at the legendary Apollo Theater amateur night, which I did. I auditioned, they liked me, and I got called with a date to perform. I sang "You're My Angel" by Anita Baker, and although I didn't win, I also didn't get booed off the stage; so that was a memorable and fulfilling experience.

The next day at school Scudder walked up to me in the hall and handed me a box of one dozen long-stem red roses and said it was from a secret admirer. I asked who it was, and he said, "If you want to meet him, he'll be here after school." So I put the roses in my locker and was trying to figure out who this person could be. Three o'clock came, I was walking to the train station, and I saw Scudder standing outside of this big black Cadillac with tinted windows. Scudder was talking to the person in the driver's seat and looking at me, so I got the feeling that might be my secret admirer in the car. As I approached the car, Scudder said, "This is him." He walked around to the passenger side, opened the back door dramatically, and said, "Meet your secret admirer," with a smile on his face. When I looked in the car, it had a white and black leather interior and looked new, a very nice car. The guy in the driver's seat said, "Hi, come on in; I don't bite. My name is Lavaba. So I see you got the roses. Hope you liked them. You sang my favorite song yesterday in the Miss Campus Contest, and you are the most beautiful young lady I have ever seen in my life. I just had to meet you. Can I give you a ride home?" I reluctantly said yes, but he seemed like a nice guy.

He engaged in some small talk. "I graduated from the school last year, and that was the first graduating class. When I heard about the contest, I had to come back and check it out because they didn't have one when I was there, and I am glad that I did." Lavaba had a great sense of humor and kept me laughing the whole ride home. His birthday was the day before mine the ninth and tenth of March; maybe that's why we hit it off so well. The ride home went by so fast I wasn't really ready for it to end, and he wasn't either, so he asked for my phone number. We exchanged numbers, and I thanked him for the ride home.

"The pleasure was all mine. I might call you later," he said.

"OK," I replied.

Shortly after I got in, the phone rang, and it was Lavaba. "Hello," I said.

"Hey, there, I can't talk long, but I wanted to know if you needed a ride home tomorrow?"

"That would be nice."

"OK then, I'll see you tomorrow. Have a good night."

"All right, you too."

I put the roses in a vase with some water and set it on the kitchen table, and then I went on to do my homework. A few hours later my dad came home and noticed the flowers immediately. "Wow, red roses. Whose are they?" "They're mine. Don't they smell good?" "Yeah, where did you get them?" "My friend from school." "What friend?"

"His name is Lavaba. He saw me sing in the Miss Campus Contest." "So what did you give him because roses are expensive? No boy is just going to give you fifty-dollar or sixty-dollar flowers for nothing. And where did he get the money? So what did you give him?"

I started crying because I couldn't believe my father was accusing me of doing something with this boy. He kept yelling at me and accusing me. I felt so hurt that I went in the bathroom, locked the door, and took some aspirin with the intention of killing myself. I lay on the floor and cried myself to sleep and woke up to my dad banging on the door, yelling at me to open the door. I knew I didn't take the whole bottle, and I was hoping five weren't going to hurt me, but he didn't know. I wanted him to feel bad for accusing me of something I didn't do. He started trying to kick the door in, so I got up and unlocked the door. He came in and saw the open bottle of pills on the floor. "What did you do to yourself?" he shouted. He was crying and telling me he loved me and that he was sorry. I hugged him and let him know I only took five aspirin. We laughed about it a little and hugged each other, and then I apologized for scaring him.

The next day, when school was over, Lavaba was there to pick me up. As soon as I got in the car, I looked him in his eyes with a stern look and told him, "You got me in trouble yesterday." Lavaba replied, "How?" I said, "Them damn *roses!*" "What happened?" Lavaba replied with concern. "My dad wanted to know what I gave you for you to spend fifty or sixty dollars on me, and where did you get the money?" "Well, did you tell him that I thought you were the most beautiful young lady I have ever seen in my life and you sang my favorite song?" "No." "Oh boy, now your dad is not going to like me." I rubbed his head and said, "You'll be all right."

Lavaba and I became good friends quickly and we found out that we had a lot in common. We both liked music, seafood, nature, movies, and being around water (not necessarily in it though). He was little in height, five foot seven, but a giant in stature, with a smooth chocolate complexion and curly hair, a real cutie pie; and after thirty years, he hasn't aged (or grown, lol) from the first day I met him. I found out how he had the money for the roses and the nice cars: his oldest brother was a drug lord. Lavaba was his assistant, and he managed the people who worked for his brother on the street.

One day Lavaba gave me a diamond ring and asked me to marry him (I guess that was a proposal), but I was still a freshman in high school, and I knew my dad would not approve of that. After the way he reacted to the roses, I would not dare walk in the house with an engagement ring on my finger. So he said he would wait and do it again when I turned eighteen. Lavaba used to tell me, "I'm going to make you my wife," but I didn't take him seriously. He would always offer to buy me nice things, and I would always refuse them. I didn't want him to think because he had money he could buy me. He always made me happy when we were in each other's company, and surprisingly, in his line of work, he lived a very clean life—no alcohol or smoking of any sort, drug free. He was an intellectual businessman at an early age. Eventually he got into the music business and started producing artists like Kool Moe Dee and Doug E. Fresh, and working with Quincy Jones, who are also advocates of clean living.

We started dating and continued for some years. Unfortunately his brother got killed, and that was a sad, hard time for Lavaba, but he got through it. We were sticking it out in our relationship, but there was something I didn't understand and it bothered me. He had developed a tendency to disappear for like three months, then come back around, and do it again. That would scare me because I didn't know what he was doing, and I didn't want him to end up like his brother, gone before his time.

When I turned sixteen, I went to Wilfred Academy for cosmetology part time to follow in my mother's and sister's profession. I graduated from the course, but I didn't take my written exam, so I just got my temporary license. My father had told my godfather that I was in beauty school, and my godfather knew a gentleman named Joe who owned a beauty shop on East Fifty-Ninth Street in Manhattan. Joe said he would give me a job at his shop when I graduated, but I had to wait until I graduated from high school to start. Well, I was in my last two years of high school and was tired of it. I was cutting class, which ultimately resulted in failure, so my counselor suggested that if I wanted to graduate on time, I needed to go to night school and summer school as well as transfer to another school to make all my credits. So that's what I did. I transferred to William

Howard Taft High School for my last year, and I did not like that because Taft was not a good school to my knowledge, but it was better than dropping out. While going to Taft, I met a guy named Jamal in the library, and he introduced me to the Islamic organization's doctrine.

Around August 28, 1987, my grandmother passed away peacefully. I was happy for her because she was starting to get dementia, and I didn't want her to suffer. With my grandmother gone and me getting ready to graduate from high school, I had to decide what I wanted to do with my life. I felt like college was a waste of money and time, so my plan was to use my trade to get a job in an influential beauty shop and become a famous person's personal beautician. I also thought about the Air Force because I wanted to travel, but that seemed kind of risky. Then I thought how I wanted to be like my grandmother and make God the focal point of my life, but how would I do that without becoming a nun?

A few times while I was out with Lavaba I would see the Muslim brothers selling oils and incense. I liked the way they smelled, so I would always buy some whenever I saw them selling some. One day I was with Lavaba and out of the blue told him I was going to join them one day. I was just talking to see what his reaction would be, and of course he thought I was joking. Finally, school was over and I graduated, but I chose not to attend the graduation because I was only at that school for a year. Lavaba said his money was acting funny, and he did another disappearing act. I went to Pennsylvania with my dad for the summer to visit his girlfriend, and that's the last I saw of Lavaba.

When I graduated, I started working at Joe's beauty shop as a shampoo girl. Joe had pictures up of all the celebrities who were clients of his. It's too many to try and name them all, but I saw a few of them in person. Surprisingly, after just a couple of weeks, he took me with him to do Miss Diana Ross's hair at her house, which was a couple of blocks from the shop. I was really surprised and honored. I just assisted him and washed her hair. Joe might have taken me with him, because the day before I mentioned to him that I was thinking about leaving and becoming a Muslim and moving into the Muslim community. I think he was trying to show me all the opportunities and possibilities of working there. I thought, what if I walked out of there and got run over by a truck? What was that job going to do for my soul? Nothing. The Islamic lifestyle seemed more focused on the creator, and that was more important to me.

Chapter 4

The Beginning

1987–1988

Ask and it shall be given you; seek and ye shall find; knock and it shall be opened unto you. (Matthew 7:7) I was seeking, precisely what, I didn't know. Purpose maybe, direction, what exactly was I created for? These questions are what led me to him. I was only eighteen and already tired of the male species and their crap. Not only speaking from my own experiences but from women in my family and friends. I decided it was time for me to get into me. I prayed about it and told God, "It appears I'm not good at choosing a mate because what I like or am attracted to is not good for me. So, Lord, I'm leaving it in your hands and asking you to choose my mate."

On my journey within, my path crossed with a young man's—not someone I found appealing, but for some reason I kept running into him at school. One day I saw him in the school library, and he struck up a conversation with me. It started out about nothing in particular, just that his name was Jamal, and he was a year younger than me; then it veered off into religion, nothing heavy, just the fundamentals. This started to happen more often as I would go to the library during my lunch break. One day he started talking about this guy he met who was selling these little books that were packed with some heavy information. I wasn't much of a reader so the books he kept talking about didn't interest me. However, due to these books, the conversations started to get interesting. He would always start out asking me some crazy question he devised from the books he read, like "Did you know that the pig was made from the cat, rat, and dog?" Now, I'm looking at him like that makes no sense and starting to wonder if he's got all his marbles. He looked like the average hip-hop teenager in the late eighties—about six foot three, kind of stocky, maybe 250 pounds, brown skin, a broad smile, full lips, and an S-curl in his afro. He said he was just getting into the "scrambling business," which is the slang term for selling drugs on street corners, but he was reconsidering that line of work because of the influence the guy he met with the books was having on him.

The guy he met was a Muslim and belonged to some community of Muslims in Brooklyn. I was familiar with these people because I would always see the men dressed in long white robes, smelling and looking so good. From time to time I would buy oils and incense from them, but I never really paid much attention to the books they sold. One day Jamal gave me one of the books to read. I said, "No, I'll pass; I told you I'm not interested, plus the book has a big red devil with a pitch fork on the cover. What is it some kind of demonic devil worship crap?" He was starting to piss me off because I didn't know what his motive was. He assured me that it wasn't devil worship so I looked over it, but I didn't like the vibe I was getting from it, and I told him exactly what he could do with his book. Jamal and I had become friends and would debate about this information. I graduated from high school and went to Harrisburg, Pennsylvania, with my dad to spend the summer with his girlfriend and her daughter, so I didn't hear any more from him.

When I got back to New York, I got a call from guess who, crazy Jamal from school. We talked and of course religion came up. He had the audacity to tell me that my grandmother wasn't going to heaven/paradise because she didn't believe in Allah. Now, you know that was a debate. My grandmother did all the things he said Muslims do to worship their god. She got up at wee hours of the morning to pray, she gave to the needy, and she read her scriptures every day. You couldn't tell me my grandmother wasn't going to heaven, and that was the end of that. The next time I heard from Jamal, he invited me to a class that the Muslim organization held every Sunday. I declined, but he insisted, saying he guaranteed the man could answer any question I had on any subject. Finally I gave in and said I'd go just to see if this was true. We set a date to go to the class, and we were to meet at the train station on 149th Street in the South Bronx. When I got to the train station, I could smell this enticing aroma that mesmerized me. As I walked farther, I saw someone in a long white robe. As I got closer, I could see it was Jamal, but he looked like a totally new being, like he had unzipped the old body and stepped out all new and improved. He was wearing a *jalabiya*, which is what the long white robes were called, and had cut off his S-curls, lost about twenty pounds, grew a beard, and was literally glowing. As I approached him, the alluring aroma filled the atmosphere. I was in awe and asked, "What is that scent you are wearing?" He replied, "Myrrh." He had become one of the Muslim brothers I would see selling oils and incense. Wow! What a transformation, and his conversations were all about the creator and his love. I was intrigued and wanted that transformation for myself.

Reflecting back on my prayer, "So, Lord, I'm leaving it in your hands and asking you to choose my mate," I thought maybe Jamal was God's selection for me. Jamal was spiritual and somewhat fanatical. One day he told me about a man he met down on Forty-Second Street in Manhattan. He said the man kind of looked like a bum, but he was selling incense. For some reason Jamal thought the man was an angel. A couple of days later, a few friends and I went down to Forty-Second Street to go to the movies, and I wanted to get some incense while I was there. I knew I would see some of the Muslim brothers there, because Forty-Second Street was a tourist site and there were always a lot of people out panhandling. If you were selling something, Forty-Second Street—really Manhattan, period—was the place to be. We went to the last show, which was over around midnight. I decided to wait until I came out of the movie to buy the incense. When I came out of the movie theater, two of the Muslim brothers were still in front of the theater selling their oils and incense and displaying them on a portable card table. One brother looked like he was packing up to leave, and the other didn't have a table but had some incense. So I asked him if he had any of the incense called "Divine Love." He said yes, but he only had one pack left, and the pack only had nineteen sticks instead of twenty. I said no problem. Then he said he would give me a discount because of the missing stick. When we exchanged the cash for the incense, I looked in his eyes to say thank you, and something told me he was the man Jamal had met, the one he thought was an angel. The next day I told Jamal I saw the angel; the fact that he gave me nineteen incense sticks got me. Muslims believe the number nineteen is a sacred number, so it kind of made sense that the angel would give me nineteen sticks of incense. I thought it might have been the man's way of letting me know who he was. Jamal was glad that I had seen the angel too, and this simple coincidence seemed to have created a bond between us. Almost every time I spoke to Jamal, he was meeting another bum that he thought was an angel. I knew it sounded crazy, but I believed him because of the experience we shared.

Jamal and I were both reading the books and studying the doctrine together. We decided we wanted to join the organization and move into the community. The guy who was converting Jamal told him if he wanted to have children and help raise the 144,000, he better get started before he moved in because once you moved in there was no telling when you would get to be with your mate. The doctrine teaches that the 144,000 are the ones spoken of in the book of Revelations who are going to be chosen to fight with the angel Michael in the last days. Since, in the community, the men, women, and children all lived in separate quarters, couples were only allowed to be together sexually at select times. This was supposed to develop self-discipline. It was believed these chosen ones would be children because they were to be pure and unadulterated. I started attending the weekly class with Jamal and eventually took my *shahada*, which was declaring the oneness of Allah, similar to being born again and accepting Jesus Christ as Lord and Savior in the Christian church. I cut off all my hair—not bald just down to the new growth to get the chemicals out; I wanted to be all natural—and I changed my name (not legally) to an Arabic name. The name changing went along with your new identity as a Muslim. Jamal and I both became vegetarians and started fasting, not because it was required but because we wanted to eat like we thought they did in the scriptures. Eventually Jamal asked me to be his mate since we were moving in the community and this was going to be the first time away from home for both of us. We started talking about helping to raise 144,000 by having a child. I wanted to have a child because, when I was thirteen, my first childhood crush led to a pregnancy, and I had to give up the baby for adoption.

Errrrrrrrr, wait! Let me go back to explain how that happened. It's getting off the subject, but it was the first crucial error I made in my life. There was a sixteen-year-old boy who was a friend of my next-door neighbor. I literally got butterflies whenever he came into my view. He was just so fine to me—curly hair, almond-shaped eyes, milk-chocolate complexion, with the cutest smile, and he could dance his butt off. To me, he resembled the actor Darnell Williams, who played the character Jessie on the soap opera *All My Children*. I was totally infatuated with him; no one ever made me feel that way. I looked older than I was and was mature for my age. Well, let's cut to the chase. One thing led to another, and we ended up having sex and I got pregnant. I know you are probably thinking, "little fast-ass girl," but it wasn't my intention to have sex. My intention was to just kiss and hump at the most. I hid the pregnancy for eight months; no one could tell that I was pregnant because I held my stomach in constantly. I thought about having an abortion in the beginning but didn't know how to go about getting one and didn't know who I could trust to help me. My cousin, who was in high school and taking some pre-nursing class, told me I couldn't have an abortion after three months. Some months had gone by, so I thought I was too far gone to have one. She also told me a story about a girl who concealed her pregnancy for the full nine months by holding her stomach in. So I decided to do that and have faith, praying I would lose the baby some way or something miraculous would happen. Then one day, seven months later, my father took me to the doctor for a pregnancy test because my grandmother told him she noticed I hadn't been getting my menses every month. The test came back negative. Whew! That was close. I just knew it was all over for me, and I couldn't figure out how the test was negative. It must have been God, I thought. Eventually I had to tell my father because I knew I would be going into labor soon. When I told my dad, he was upset and disappointed in me, but he was supportive. He said it hurt him that I had to go through the whole thing by my-self. He took me back to the same doctor to be examined and asked him why the test had come back negative if I was pregnant. The doctor said after seven months a pregnancy test done with urine wouldn't show accurate results. My dad did not feel it would be in my or the baby's best interest to keep him. So when the baby was born, I had to give him up for adoption. A beautiful baby boy, born January 25, 1983, that we named Bruce after my father's brother. By accident I got a chance to see my baby for a hot minute be-fore a nurse realized I wasn't supposed to see him because I was giving him up for adoption. I didn't want to give him up, because after nine months of carrying him, I had fallen in love with him. However, I knew it would probably be best to give him to a family that would be better equipped to raise him. For years I dealt silently with the pain I felt for giving him up, wondering if he was with a good family, safe, and being loved.

A couple of weeks passed, and Jamal and I decided to attempt to get pregnant. I wasn't really sexually attracted to him, but I was attracted to his love for Allah and his desire to learn all he could about Allah, but we had to have sex to get pregnant. He came over to my apartment one late afternoon when my dad was at work and I was home alone. We sat on the rug in the living room, talked, and listened to Stevie Wonder's album *The Secret Life of Plants*, along with Luther, Anita, and some other albums I liked. The sun was going down, and nature set the perfect ambiance to get us in the mood. Since I wasn't really attracted to him, it was kind of hard to get things started, not to mention he was well endowed. We kissed and fondled each other just long enough to get it in because there was no chemistry between us, in my opinion. It may sound sacrilegious, but the whole time we were doing it, I was praying to get pregnant and chanting the names of Allah. There was no pleasure involved, but we got through it. When we finished, I found out the feeling was mutual and he was praying too. I feared I wouldn't be able to have another child because I gave my first child away. So I prayed that Allah would bless me with another little boy. The next month came, and I didn't get my menses. Yes! Allah had answered my prayer. I was pretty confident that we succeeded because my menses was always on time.

A few weeks later we finally got accepted to move into the community. Jamal had requested that we move to a community that was just getting started, instead of the main branch in Brooklyn. We were instructed to move into the community in Baltimore, Maryland. On February 14, 1988, my father took us to the bus terminal, and before we got on the bus, he asked if we wanted anything to take with us to eat. "Yes," we replied. "Just a Kaiser roll with some butter." My father reminds me of that to this day. "What were you all thinking about?" It was humility; we were practicing humility. So we went to Baltimore, and it wasn't bad; in fact it was rather nice. It was more suburban, more trees and green grass. When we arrived at the

ALEX P. MIDORI

Baltimore community, while we were trying to be humble eating bread and butter, the amir told us he had just finished eating a steak dinner. The amir was the title of the person who led the congregation, and if he was married, his wife is called the amira. When we arrived, I was the only woman other than the amira. The building I was to reside in was a three-story building adjoining another identical building. The apartment they put us in had no electricity and no furniture, just a stove and refrigerator. There was no food, and we had no money, but Jamal went out to see if he could hustle up something. When he returned, he had a bag full of groceries. I asked him how he got all the food. He said he ran into some angels, and they told him the baby and I needed certain things to eat. They just started putting things in his basket and got it for us. It was enough stuff to hold us over for a few days or so because we didn't eat much anyway. Jamal went out and got candles, some milk crates, a slab of plywood, and a small foam mattress from the brothers. He placed the plywood on top of the milk crates and the foam on top of the wood. I laid my sleeping bag on the foam and got comfortable. It wasn't the pull-out mattress on the couch that I was accustomed to sleeping on at home, but it was better than the bare floor. While Jamal was out gathering the bedding, he said the brothers told him he wouldn't be staying with me; he had to stay with the brothers. He said he just let them talk, but he was not leaving me in that apartment without any electricity all night by myself.

At dawn, the sky was dark and still. The captivating call

to Morning Prayer was being played throughout the community over a loudspeaker. We made *wudu*, which is the preparation for prayer that consists of washing the hands, head, forearms, face, nose, mouth, and feet with water, and then we prayed. After prayer I went to take my bath. While I was in the tub, I heard the front door burst open with a loud *boom!* and boots stomping down the hall toward the bathroom. My heart dropped, and I said to myself, "I know they're not coming in here." The boots kept going past the bathroom to the bedroom. Then I heard yelling and tussling as they left the room and came down the hall toward the bathroom. Jamal yelled out, "Don't worry, Candace." Then the sounds continued down the hall and out the door. I hurried up and got out of the tub and got dressed so, in case they decided to come back, I'd be ready for them. Thank goodness, no one came back. Later on that afternoon, Jamal came back. He was a little bruised up. "Jamal, what happened to you?" I asked.

"The brothers jumped on me because I stayed here with you last night, and I'm going to stay here tonight too. They think I'm going to leave you here with them lurking around…I don't think so."

On the ground floor of the building was a bookstore owned by the organization, and behind the store was the masjid, which is a prayer area for the congregation. It was time for afternoon prayer. Jamal and I got there early to read and chant before prayer. As the brothers were coming in, Jamal told me to watch how they set up the ranks for prayer. The ranks were supposed to start from left to right, so the first person to come in was supposed to sit on the far left and the next person on the right of him and so on and so forth. As the brothers came in, they sat wherever they felt like sitting, without order or formation. After prayer we went outside and Jamal said, "You saw that, right? Jinns! They are a bunch of jinns." Then he said a few of the brothers were crows. We would see these crows flying around sometimes, and he said he noticed that whenever the crows were around he wouldn't see certain brothers. Then, whenever the brothers were around, he wouldn't see any crows. Wooow…I just left that alone; it was a little too heavy for me. The doctrine taught that men were more spiritual than women so I thought, maybe because of that, he could see things I couldn't see, and I left it at that. While we were sitting outside, Jamal was staring at the ground, and I said,

"What are you looking at?"

He said, "An ant." There was an ant crawling on the concrete carrying a big crumb. "You see that crumb? If Allah will provide for that ant, you don't think he will provide for us?"

I said yes, and Jamal said, "He is the provider." Allah has one hundred attributes/names and one of them is The Provider. The more I watched that ant, the more I thought of the greatness of Allah. The ant appears to have no purpose or significance in life if you just happen to notice one crawling around aimlessly, yet the creator provides for it and all other creatures that we think we are superior to. I knew Jamal brought that ant to my attention so I wouldn't worry about the fact that we only had enough food to last us for a few days, or maybe Allah brought it to our attention to say, "Don't worry, I've got your back."

The amir, also known as Raqi, and his wife, Raqiya, were going to New York to pick up some supplies for the bookstore, so they told us they would be gone for a few days. I thought, sarcastically, "OK, great, now I'm going to be the only female in this place." That didn't sit too well with me; after all, I really didn't know any of these people, and Jamal was outnumbered at about six to one. Then I thought, "These guys are all Muslims. I should be all right...on second thought, Muslim or not, they are still men and I don't trust them. I'll just pray about it." I knew I would be faced with obstacles put in my way by Satan in his attempts to take me off the path. Therefore, I didn't want to be so easily deterred.

My facial expression must have been revealing my thoughts because Raqiya said, "There's a young lady named Haliyma who's waiting to be accepted so she can move in. She stops by every now and then to help out, and she'll be staying with you until we get back. Speaking of her, here she is now." With a sigh of relief, I replied, "Thank you, because I really didn't want to be here alone." "Candace, I wouldn't leave you here by yourself, but I didn't think anyone would do anything to you. Raqi and I have known these brothers for years." Raqiya was a very intelligent, straightforward, and down-to-earth sister. If there was someone I should watch out for, I believe she wouldn't leave him there with me. Haliyma stepped in, an attractive, full-figured, fair-skinned sister with two children, "As salaamu alaykum, sisters," she said with a pleasant smile. "Wa alaykum as salaam," we replied. We chatted for a while and got familiar; this weekend might not be so bad after all.

It was after ten o'clock; Haliyma and I were just getting the kids to sleep when we heard a loud knocking at the door. Haliyma answered the door. It was Jamal, so I went to the door. "Oh my God, what happened to you?" I said in terror. When I got to the door, Jamal was standing there drenched in blood. "The brothers tried to kill me. They jumped me and stomped on me with them damn combat boots, and when I made it to my feet, I tried to get out the door but it was locked. The next thing I know, one of them was coming at me with a machete, so I kicked through the glass door. As I was getting out of the door, he hit me in the back of my head with the machete. I need you to come with me; they won't do anything with you there." So I went with him. He was out of breath and kind of faint, staggering down the stairs in front of me, his white jalabiya now red with blood. I got a weird feeling in the pit of my stomach that I had never felt before. Whether it was fear or anxiety or a combination of the two, I didn't know what I was about to walk into. "Would they try to kill the both of us?" I thought. "I don't know, but I do know I can't just leave him out there alone. If they're going to do something, they're going to have to do us both. I trust in Allah." That weird feeling in my stomach turned into confidence, I felt like no matter what happened, everything was going to be OK, no fear. When we got outside the building, I saw a few brothers in front of the store cleaning up the broken glass. They were really mad because they had just put that door in, and they acted like Jamal was going to have to pay for it. One of the brothers walked over to us and said they had called the amir and he wanted to speak to me. Jamal said to me, "If they say I have to leave, I want you to stay because it'll be best for you and the baby; I'll work my way back, OK?" We walked up to the bookstore, and I saw the brother with the machete, doing a bad job of concealing it; he was a West Indian brother walking around looking like a maniac. Jamal said to me, "He's the one who hit me with the machete." He looked our way as he walked by, but he didn't make eye contact. Then it dawned on me that he was one of the brothers Jamal said was a crow. See, this animosity from the brothers toward Jamal had been building up for a few days now. We had been there for about five days, and almost every day Jamal was getting into something with them because he was telling them what he thought of them. So there was a possibility they did have intentions of killing him, but he got away. We walked in the store, and the brother gave me the phone. "Candace, are you OK?"

"Yes, I'm fine."

"Well, we should be there tomorrow, and we'll talk then. I just wanted to make sure you were all right. OK, we'll see you tomorrow."

"All right." I passed the phone back to the brother, and he continued to talk. I told Jamal what Raqi said and we left the store. Jamal walked me to the apartment. I felt bad for him and I was worried because he had to sleep with those brothers. I didn't know if he was going to make it through the night. I had a hard time sleeping because I kept having visions of him bleeding to death or the brothers attacking him in his sleep. It was like the devil was tormenting me with each vivid thought. I kept calling on the names of Allah until I finally fell asleep.

The next morning was gloomy and overcast, no sunshine to lift my spirits after a horrible night. Jamal came to the door, still wearing the same blood-stained clothes. I was glad to see he made it through the night safely. "How are you feeling this morning?" I asked.

"I'm doing all right, all praises due to Allah. Let's go for a walk to the park."

"You know where a park is?" I asked.

"No, we could follow the birds," Jamal replied.

"Follow the birds? I know you're crazy now. How are the birds going to lead us to the park, Jamal?"

"Do you want to go or not? Where's your faith?" I thought about it for a minute. We had to wait for Raqi to get back from New York anyway, and it would be better than sitting around with the jinns. "OK, let's go." And we were on our way. Amazingly, there was a group of birds flying above us. We walked for a few blocks, still following the birds, and came upon a big open field; it looked like a golf course the way the grass was so neatly manicured. In the middle of this field was a big, beautiful oak tree. The first thing that came to my mind was the tree in the Garden of Eden. It was around five thirty and the sky was changing; it seemed as though the clouds opened up and the sun had come out just for us to watch it set. The colors in the sky

were so spectacular; it was indescribable. I felt such grati-
tude to Allah for the blessings. Tears filled my eyes, and I
felt as if that beauty was a gift to us from the Most High
for our faithfulness and a comfort to us after the hardship.
It was time for evening prayer, so we hurried back.

Later on that evening, Raqi and Raqiya returned from
New York. I was a little nervous because I didn't know
what they were going to say about the whole situation.
They called us to the bookstore to have our discussion. I
guess they had already heard the brothers' side of the story
because none of the brothers were present. Jamal explained
himself, but it looked to me like they already had their
minds made up. "Well, we're sorry to say it, but, Jamal, you
will have to leave due to your reckless behavior. Now, we're
going to have to purchase another door, which we really
can't afford. Candace, you are welcome to stay if you want;
it's up to you." "I'll stay," I replied. I felt so bad for Jamal
because he didn't have anywhere to go. I knew he didn't
want to go back home; his home was pretty dysfunctional.
As Jamal was leaving, I told him to go straight to the hospital to get stitched up before he went anywhere else. "OK,
Candace, I'll do that, and don't worry about me, just take
care of the baby. I'll be all right." We hugged and said our
good-byes.

With Jamal gone, I kind of felt alone, but I adjusted.
Haliyma moved in, and we got along pretty well. Every
day I cleaned the masjid and bookstore and then helped
with the kids. This went on for three months, and then one
day Raqiya told me I had to move to New York. "Why?" I

asked. "Because your mate wants to move back in, and he has to come back through Baltimore first. It's up to you whether you want to go with him." This was a hard decision for me to make because Jamal and I were just friends. I wasn't in love with him and didn't want to spend the rest of my life with him. However, I thought Allah may have chosen him for me, so I didn't want to go against that. I prayed and cried about it all night and decided to move back to New York with him. Once Jamal got to Baltimore, Raqiya let me know he was there. When I saw him, I got that same feeling in the pit of my stomach I had the night he came to me all bloody. I really didn't want to leave with him, but I thought it was a test of faith, so I stepped out on faith and went with him.

Chapter 5
New York: The Teacher

**I never imagined I'd meet this mystical
man, leader of thousands of followers**

When we arrived in New York, we were directed to our
living quarters. Jamal was escorted to the brother's
quarters, which were in a different building. With a duffel
bag on my shoulder and a sleeping bag under my other arm,
I was directed to the living quarters for the new sisters; it
was located in a three-family brownstone. Each floor of the
house had six rooms, one full bath, and a kitchen. The first
room, which was the biggest, slept about fifteen women, and
I was assigned a spot in that room. With that many women
in one room, you might think it would be messy, but it was
quite the contrary. Each sister had her own little radius to
set up her sleeping gear. The floors were parquet and im-
maculate; I was surprised and impressed. Sad to say, being
around that many women, I was anticipating some static
from someone because that was what I usually encountered
since childhood, with these hazel eyes. Some females would
dislike me without even getting to know me. Surprisingly,
everyone seemed to be nice, and I was grateful for that
because I am not a fighter by nature. It seemed like God
would always place people in my life who were fighters, and
they would look out for me. The house was pretty empty

because everyone was at their job sites, which were located in different buildings. By around seven or eight o'clock that night, everybody started coming in from work, and it got kind of loud. Most of the sisters were between seventeen and twenty-five, so you can imagine what it sounded like. Nonetheless I was happy to be there.

I met Marcus about three days after being in the Brooklyn community. I was assigned to work in the mail room shipping department which was located right on the other side of his personal office. Now, I wasn't a Marcus groupie like Jamal; I just liked the doctrine. The weirdest thing happened to me though. Prior to ever even seeing Marcus, I had two dreams about him. In the first dream, I was walking to the train station at night. As I approached the stairs leading down into the station, a bald black man with a thin ponytail sat Indian style on a mat at the entrance of the station. He was dressed in what looked like a black jalabiya with his eyes closed. I continued past him and down into the station, and then I woke up. In the second dream, I was in a hallway with a nice-looking, brown-skinned man with curly hair. I told him I wanted my hair in curls, and he said he would do it for me; then I was in a barber's chair, and he was rolling my hair with rods. I remember waking up and thinking, "That was a weird dream and who was that man? He seemed familiar, but I didn't recognize him."

Before I met Marcus in person, I had a reverence and compassion for him just from reading his books. When I would look at his pictures, his eyes seemed like they spoke to my soul; it was like I could feel his pain. When I would think about the job he had, getting his people from out of the muck and mire, it seemed as if he was carrying the whole world on his shoulders. I felt so sorry for him and wanted to help him carry that load in any way I could. The more pictures I saw of him as Dr. Roark (his stage name) and the multiple personalities he claimed to have as an avatar (the physical embodiment of an idea or concept, a personification; in Hinduism the incarnation of a deity), which he claimed to be, I realized that he was the man I had dreamed about. It didn't explain the dreams, but at least I knew who the two men in the dreams were…him.

One day, one of his mates named Martha came in the office and asked me if I knew how to do hair. I told her, "Yes, I went to cosmetology school when I was sixteen." She asked me if I would do Dr. Roark's hair because he had a show. I was nervous but so happy to be of some help. I followed her in the house, and she led me to the bathroom, which was huge. The bathroom had a professional barber's chair, shampoo bowl, and plenty of mirrors and lights. In the corner of the room, an area for bathing was sectioned off with a big, black, round Jacuzzi tub that could hold at least five or six people comfortably. I was amazed because I had never seen a bathroom like that except on television. Everything was black and gold: black carpet, gold faucet, black sink, and a big TV and stereo component, it was like a movie. Having lived in South Bronx most of my life, I had never seen anything like this before, so I was impressed to say the least.

Marcus came in the bathroom dressed very casually in a thin white cotton, dashiki-type top with matching bottoms, and he asked Martha to leave and close the door behind her. I felt special to be alone with him because there was always a group of people around him. Surprisingly, as nervous as I was, I could still function normally. Being around him felt so good. He kept me laughing the whole time we were together; he even laughed at a few of my corny jokes. I wanted that feeling to go on forever. During those few hours I was with him alone, it was like no one else existed, referring to the other women. Even though I saw Marcus as superior to me with all his knowledge and years of wisdom (according to his doctrine he had 36 trillion years of knowledge), I could feel my concern for him turning into love. This wasn't a lustful love but a genuine love.

Every week the community would have a family meeting where everything that was going on in the community would be discussed. If anyone wasn't living up to his or her obligations, be it work related or marital problems, this is when all the cards were put on the table, so to speak. These meetings were televised throughout the community, so if you got called out, it could be rather embarrassing to say the least. I told myself and Jamal that I would not tolerate being embarrassed like that in a public meeting. The brothers had to meet a daily quota of one hundred dollars. Each week at the family meetings, they would announce the names of the brothers who didn't meet their quota. After that announcement those brothers were asked individually why they didn't make their quota. Needless to say, the meetings would get a little heated at times when people had to explain why they couldn't make their quota, which would provide for their families' food and utilities. Unfortunately the day came when Jamal's name was called. Oh, I was pissed off, and I meant what I said when I told him I wasn't tolerating it. We talked about it, and he had some lame excuse. I didn't break it off with him; I just decided to discuss it with Marcus the next time I saw him.

The next day, I saw Marcus and asked him if I could talk to him when he had the time. He said, "We can talk now, follow me." We went in his house and he said, "It's a nice day; let's sit outside." I was wondering how we were going to do that since we were walking further into his house. We went up a spiral staircase that led to another apartment with a patio. The patio was actually on the roof of this two-story brownstone and was decked out just like the rest of the apartment, with a movie screen, stereo sound system, and colorful artificial vines and flowers. Andreas Vollenweider was playing softly on the stereo; it was so serene I felt as if I had walked into another dimension. I wasn't spaced out or anything; it just didn't feel like I was on Heart Street in Brooklyn, New York. Marcus sat across from me and asked, "What color are your eyes?"

I replied, "Hazel."

"Oh, you got them funny color eyes."

I smiled, and he said, "So what did you want to talk about?"

"Well, let me make a long story short. The brother

Jamal is my mate, and I don't think the relationship is going to work."

"Why do you think that?"

"When we got here, I told him I wouldn't tolerate him being irresponsible, because I could do badly by myself. So if he can't make his quota, it's not going to work."

"How old is he?"

"A year younger than me, seventeen," I replied.

"That's the problem right there. First of all, you shouldn't be able to talk to him like that. Right now, you can't do anything because you're pregnant; you have to wait until after you have the baby." That's not what I wanted to hear.

On the first day at my job in the mail room shipping department, the door to Marcus's personal office flew open, and all I saw was a white jalabiya fly by. It happened so quickly it startled me. It startled me because I knew it had to have been a brother, and I didn't have my veil up. Brothers are supposed to announce themselves before entering a room where sisters are, and the brother who came through the door didn't announce himself. I thought that was very rude. I also noticed that none of the other sisters seemed to be bothered by it, so I asked why, and they said, "That was Marcus. We don't have to put our veils up around him." I felt so foolish. It didn't even dawn on me that I was right in front of his office, but I didn't anticipate him coming through the door that fast either. Every day Marcus would make his rounds through the offices, and at some point he would stop in my work area and talk to us. He would talk about things like people being spinsters. According to the dictionary, a spinster is a woman who has remained unmarried beyond the conventional age for marriage in her culture or society. To my recollection, he explained a spinster as someone who was afraid to take chances and experience life by living out their fantasies, for example, sexual fantasies. This made me think and ask myself, "Do I have any fantasies?" He asked that, and I couldn't really think of any so that made me feel kind of spinsterish. Most of us had the same reaction, like I never really thought about it and was basically too shy to talk about any thoughts of sex. I think that was his way of getting prepared for that week's question-and-answer class. It was very informative as well as a privilege to be around him.

Marcus had many mates, both "wives" and "concubines." I know you're probably thinking what's the difference? Well, a mate is a partner, and a man with status (which he had) was entitled to have more than one mate. A wife is a man's partner in marriage, legal or common law. A concubine, also called a courtesan, is a woman who cohabits with an important man (which he was).

When it was time to meet the family, i.e., his wives, I was kind of excited and nervous at the same time. I didn't know what to expect; the reality of this was all new to me. You know, women can be very catty. This was also my first time in Marcus's house, which everyone didn't have the privilege to experience, so I felt honored. His living quarters were in a big brownstone building where he had all of his offices. See, Marcus was an entrepreneur, and basically this whole neighborhood was his enterprise, so to speak, or what we called "the community." He had several businesses/productions and about eighteen brownstones that housed all the local members, which included workers, builders, children, and propagators of the doctrine. Out of these eighteen buildings, about four of them he resided in at different times, and each time he moved he would leave his "old baggage" behind, old baggage being original mates/ wives. As new wives were added to the "stable," he would move select ones into his new spot. Each group was a little younger than the last. At this time he was living in the building where all of his offices were. One day, while in the office working, I was invited to Marcus's house after work by one of his wives, Martha.

Martha was older than me, probably in her midthirties, tall and slender but hippy, very attractive, mild mannered, and unintimidating. When work was over, Martha came and escorted me to Marcus's house. As I walked in, I entered a bright kitchen with red walls and a black-and-white tile floor. The wall directly in front of the entrance was mirrored, so you could see yourself and anyone behind you as you walked in. To my left was a circular doorway that led to the living room.

The living room was black and gold: black carpet, black walls with gold borders, and one wall decorated with white

limestone, enclosing a fifty-two-inch, wide-screen television
and entertainment center. Now this was the late eighties,
so that TV was huge to me. Once in the living room, to
the right was an elevated circular platform, which was his
bed. (As Muslims we slept on the floor.) The platform was
covered with a thick sheepskin rug and a beautiful $2,000
comforter set in black and gold, of course. The bed was en-
closed by a sheer lace black and gold canopy that hung from
the ceiling (at least it looked like to me). To the left was a
gold spiral staircase leading up to another bedroom, living
room, kitchen, dining area, and patio. In the living room,
to my surprise, were all his wives. Everyone appeared to
get along well, so I was happy. I also felt grateful to Allah
for blessing me with another family because I had made
the sacrifice of leaving my biological family to move into
the community. The doctrine taught that family was those
who believed as you believed.

Chapter 6
Polygamy

The practice of having more than one spouse at the same time No games, no lies; it is what it is

Growing up, marriage was something I did not believe in; it just didn't seem to ever work, at least not in my generation and a few generations before mine. I knew a couple who shacked up for ten years with no apparent problems, but, as soon as they decided to tie the knot, he decided to have an affair—and better yet he messed up and got caught. Why? It's almost like the institution of marriage has a curse on it. Actually, the more I think about it, it's not the institution of marriage with the curse, but the morals and statutes of the individuals. When I decided to become a Muslim, people would say to me, "You know they believe in having more than one wife." That didn't bother me; in fact I applauded it because I didn't believe a man could be loyal to one woman anyway. At least in polygamy you knew who all your partners were—no lies, no games, it is what it is, take it or leave it— as long as he could provide for all of them.

One afternoon another girl and I were at Marcus's house cleaning or something. Really I think he kind of just enjoyed having us around for any reason. Out of the blue he handed the other girl a beautiful diamond ring and asked her what she thought of it. She said, "It's gorgeous, whose is it?" He handed it to me and said, "Hers." Oh my goodness! I was flabbergasted. Honestly I thought he was giving it to her or somebody else but definitely not me. I'd just met him. I could tell she was upset and surprised as well, but what could she say? Of course that caused some hard feelings between the girl and me. The word that I got that ring spread like wildfire, and people were mad. Some women had been there for years and never got a ring. Who the hell was I? His original/first mates had rings, but this was something new, me getting a ring so early in the relationship. I started spending more time around Marcus between doing his hair and helping to clean his home. People didn't like that and acted like they couldn't understand why or how I got to spend so much time with him. I don't know why they just couldn't accept me being with him, because there was always a main wife that he had around him the most. Some of them went as far as to say that I must have put a spell on him because my mother was Jamaican. To add fuel to their fire, he told me I could move into one of his personal houses, and when the baby was due, I could have the baby delivered there. Wow! That was special and unexpected. There had been other home deliveries but only a few, to my knowledge.

I can recall the first time I spent the night at Marcus's house. There were two other girls with me, I'll say around my age, seventeen or eighteen. We were called to his house by one of his mates and asked if we wanted to spend some time with him. Of course we accepted the invitation. It was more than a privilege to spend time with Marcus or even just to be in his presence.

We arrived at his house shortly after work, which was around eight or nine that evening. I had no idea why I was asked to come to his house, but I didn't question the offer. I could remember feeling a little nervous and taken aback but at the same time so excited. This was how I normally felt when I was around him. The other two girls seemed overly happy while I just kept my emotions suppressed inside.

We all got comfortable sitting on some big throw pillows he had laid out on the rug in his living room as we watched a movie. The movie ended and the lights were completely out, so I figured he was either tired or it was time for us to go. He turned on some soft music and the vibe was so serene; I thought he was probably meditating or having some deep mystical thoughts. I closed my eyes in hopes of connecting with him in my mind and chanted over and over the names of Allah giving thanks (in my head of course). I was so grateful to be in his presence. I really felt honored to be with him. I kept chanting and concentrating on connecting with his thoughts. As I opened my eyes, I noticed a blinking red light coming from the stereo component. The light continued to blink, which left me a little befuddled only because I hadn't noticed it blinking since I had been lying there.

As my eyes adjusted to the dark, I put all my focus on this light. I was looking at it…and looking at it… The more

I focused on it, the better I could see that something was moving back and forth in front of the light. This was what was making the light appear to be blinking. Like a curious cat, I really started to put all my attention on this light, and as my eyes adjusted, I could see it was someone's head bobbing up and down. Huh? I gasped with shock. To my surprise one of the girls was giving him oral sex. I could not believe this was happening! Here I was thinking this was some type of spiritual occasion, and he was lying there getting a damn blow job.

Still shocked out of my mind, I lay there tense and nervous. What started out as a simple blow job developed into a ménage à trois as I started to hear and feel motion from the girl who was lying next to me. I thought to myself, something is about to go down. I started to hear slurps and smacking, which was really getting me upset. Technically I really didn't have any reason to get ticked off because it wasn't like he was my man or anything, but I just didn't think it was that kind of party, and I really didn't expect to see that side of him.

The more I thought about it as I listened to all the quiet sounds, I began to feel disrespected and kind of violated— not to mention I was about six months pregnant at the time with my oldest son. Therefore, I had no intention of joining this little sexcapade. I started feeling angry but also stimulated for some odd reason. I guess the stimulation was due to the sounds I could hear from the three of them. These emotions were conflicting within me, creating an energy that was fierce in the pit of my stomach.

With all this action going on, I decided to get up and leave. I guess he heard me get up because he asked me if I was OK. I replied yes. He then said, "Well, you could lie on the bed; that should be more comfortable for you." I went and lay on the bed, closed my eyes, and tried to go to sleep, but all I could do was cry my eyes out. I felt so hurt listening to them having sex. I know I could have just gotten up and left, but I didn't want to ruin my chances of ever being around him again. He basically made it clear in his conversations with us in the office that he had no inhibitions, and he liked people who were the same way. I guess the purpose of me being there that night was so he could see how I would react to that scenario. Part of me wished I was freaky enough to join in without thinking twice about it, because it seemed like that was probably the type of woman he liked. However, I did the absolute contrary and freaked out internally, feeling like I was just crazy. My inquisitiveness and plain ole human nature made me dry my eyes and watch their naked silhouettes grind and intertwine. I wanted to see how he was going to do this because it was new to me. The scene got increasingly intense, and the sounds of sex got louder and louder as the grinding turned into strong thrusts. Just when I thought it was over, they changed positions, and it was like they started all over again. After a while it seemed like it would never end. Eventually, I fell asleep and Marcus awoke me with a kiss on my forehead. "Hey, sleepyhead, how are you doing?"

"All right," I replied with a slight attitude.

"Aw, it'll be your turn soon," he said with a snicker. I was still mad, but I was glad it was over. The two other girls giggled as they went to get a warm rag to clean him and some cold ginseng tonic to quench his thirst. I felt awkward, like I didn't fit in, and I wondered how the girls felt about having sex with him in front of each other, but I didn't feel comfortable asking them. After everyone was all washed up, we all lay in the bed talking about work and anything else that came up. As we talked I felt a little better, and Marcus kept cracking jokes about the girls so we laughed until we drifted off to sleep. That was my introduction to the sexual aspect of polygamy, I guess.

The next time I was with him it was just Martha and I. We started the evening watching a movie or something educational, like a documentary on various cultures or extraterrestrials, as he did some writing. After a while he asked me to fix him some tea, so I went in the kitchen to do that. When I brought him the tea, I didn't see Martha and thought, "Whaaaat? We're alone." I was nervous because I didn't want to bore him, but it turned out OK. He wasn't hard to talk to like I thought he might be with all his knowledge and wisdom. In fact he was the total opposite. He made me feel very comfortable; he was down to earth, and his sense of humor was enormous. When the movie was over, he told me to run his tub, and I could take a bath if I wanted to when he finished. When I was through bathing, I went back in the room, and he was lying on his back on the bed. "Would you like your feet massaged?" I asked.

"Yes indeedy," he replied. We snuggled, and I got some oil and started massaging his feet. Well into the message I heard snoring, so I lay down next to him. He woke up, or just stopped snoring, and started fondling me softly, separating my thighs and sliding his hands down in between them as he proceeded to bring me to a climax. As I tried to gather myself and lift my head up from hanging off the edge of the bed, I heard something that sounded like someone moving around on the other side of the room. "What was that?" I asked disconcertedly. "Oh, that's just Martha. She asked if she could shack out over there on the pillow. It's all right." I was really surprised, embarrassed, and a little perturbed because he could have let me know she was there. I was making all kinds of noises and trying to climb the wall on the opposite side of the room while still on my back, which was impossible, but I was trying to get there (chuckle). He calmed my nerves and explained to me that some people are voyeurs; they get pleasure from watching. I guess that was better than Martha just joining in, because I would have felt uncomfortable. It was my first time being intimate with him after knowing him for nine months or so. Awkward.

Chapter 7
The "Cult"

Never thought it could happen to me

Brainwashing is something I never believed in. I thought it was something bored, weak-minded people made up. I depended on Marcus for everything. I looked up to him in a way that one should be looking up to God. It wasn't something that happened overnight; it took some time. It felt as though Marcus was the keeper of my soul, and I personally handed it over to him. I had no say in how my life should be handled or led. In my eyes I had become useless, and there was nothing else left for me to accomplish. I believed Marcus was my soul mate and all God had in store for me. It kind of felt as though I let God down by making what seemed a god out of a man of the flesh. Subconsciously I worshiped Marcus, and all I could do was visualize him. I just wanted to please him. When you are in love, you manage to find a good excuse to do wrong things. I was willing and desired to surrender my divinity to become one with the man I loved, believed in, and totally trusted. You have to understand, this love was no ordinary love because he was no ordinary man. This man wore many hats, so to speak. He was my spiritual guide, my teacher, my boss, my lover, my confidant, and my buddy (he could also have been my daddy as he was twenty-five years my senior). I didn't realize at the time that in doing this I was losing myself, my identity, my individuality, my mind, and my soul because it was all about him. As his mate or "wife," I thought we were supposed to become one. Gradually I depended on him for everything. Hell, I really didn't have a choice; he ran the show. I had nothing, I owned nothing, and I thought he could read my mind.

One day I felt really frustrated and hopeless, so I told Marcus I felt like I was taking up space that someone who was business minded could be filling. And he said, "No, everyone is not business minded. Some people are domesticated, and that's what you are, so you can make my tea, cook, and help clean up." He had showed me how he liked his tea, and when I made it, he liked it better than anyone else's tea. (If you're wondering, yes, he drinks a lot of tea. He says it's part of his eastern culture.) So I would be in the office working, and he would call out for me to come and make him a cup of tea at any time of the day or night. At any time I'd then make him a cup of tea and end up being in his house for a while doing other things, like cleaning up. One thing would lead to another as far as taking care of him and his dwelling. I didn't mind; I liked it. I didn't see anything wrong with it. I think where I made my mistake was that after a few years of working in the office and dealing with the business aspect of things, I was doing domestic work, but you still had to have an active role in the office or all the other women would look down on you (jealousy). They were already picking at me because he liked me so they would just look for stuff or create stuff—for example,

"Oh, she don't wash her clothes on the regular" or "Oh, she's stupid" and she's this and she's that. They would even say that I was a recessive gene because my eyes were light (duh! that's what makes them light). They did everything they could to try to dirty me up in his eyes. It was OK though because I wasn't thinking about them. I was focused on the Most High and Marcus, that's it. I was doing whatever I could to please him and help him with his job because his job was getting the word (doctrine) out and getting the information to the people. I wanted to help because I felt like I was helping God's mission. I thought it was God's work, and I was helping Marcus help God (like God Almighty needs help). So how could I go wrong?

In the beginning he would have talks in the office about staff members with bad money management skills and issues like that. He also talked about being a spinster and not living your life to the fullest as far as speaking your mind and doing whatever you wanted to do, living out your fantasies. Then it started getting sexual. At first it was just about freeing your mind: don't have any inhibitions, just be who you are, strive to be who you want to be, and enjoy life. At the same time, we were praying five times a day, fasting, and doing all the things that you're supposed to do, according to Islam, so I felt like, wow, this was really great. This was how life was supposed to be lived. I was looking forward to being all that I was supposed to be, not being shy, and not holding back my thoughts or anything. Marcus would say, "How many of us have fulfilled our fantasies? Think about what you would like to do." So that had me thinking, "Well, dang, what would I like to do? I don't really know because that's not something I really thought about." I don't want it to seem like this is all about sex or perversions, but that played a role in it. He made it clear that he liked people who basically didn't have any inhibitions, just free spirits, I guess. Inhibitions, wherever they were in your life, held you back, starting from something personal like your sexual fantasies and desires or whatever. That thought pattern held you back in life because it was fear, fear of being yourself. I thought that that was what he was trying to accomplish: getting us out of that fearful mind-set so we could be who we really are or who we were intended to be. I didn't see myself as a freak or "inhibition-less." I didn't have much experience in the fantasizing department so I didn't think that I fell into that category, but I wanted to be somebody that he enjoyed being around. For a while it seemed like we weren't really that compatible…well, not the way he was with some of his other mates. I didn't have the skills or whatever it was that they had, in my opinion. They were all older than me. I was by that time nineteen, and most of his other mates were in their late twenties to early forties, so I felt kind of nerdy or like the spinster he called people who didn't really go all out. However, I was willing to learn, and I guess that was one of the areas where I made my mistake in trying to please him and do whatever he wanted.

Chapter 8

Incarceration

"Do not worry." (Matthew 6:24–34)

If someone would have told me twenty-five years ago that I was going to be incarcerated at the age of thirty-three, I would have told them, "You a liar before God." Life takes so many twists and turns, you can't predict how your life is going to be twenty-five years from now or even tomorrow.

Being incarcerated was an enlightening experience for me, to say the least. It was another opportunity for me to turn to the Most High for guidance and strength. Starting from the arrest, I had no idea why we were being arrested or what lay ahead, but I knew I had to depend on God and put my trust and faith in him. I had no one there with me—not daddy, mommy, or my companion (hell, he was locked up too). The Holy Spirit comforted me by softly saying to my spirit, "It's going to be all right," and I had no worries. The only worrying I did was for others. I do have to say when I got to prison, the devil attacked me by way of fear. I can't even tell you exactly what I was afraid of. All I know is it had taken over my entire body, and just like in the cartoons, my body trembled with fear. I couldn't control it. My teeth chattered, my hands trembled; thank God the only thing I didn't do was urinate on myself. I was visibly terrified. One of the biggest women in that room started laughing at me and said, "You scared?" I just looked away and did my best to remain expressionless. I thought I was keeping it together, but by her reaction it was obvious that I was scared, and this was involuntary. I already knew that God had my back because he gave me peace while I was in the county jail for seven months (which they didn't give me credit for by the way).

When I got to prison, it was another level in the faith department. Like the TV show, *So You Think You Can Dance?* this was *So You Think You Got Faith?* Let's see how you do in the pit. When I got to the state prison for diagnostics, it was like a dark cloud hovered over, around, and all through the place, including the people. The first thing they do is dehumanize you by screaming and yelling in your face, and you better not look them in the eye because they'll put you on blast. "You eyeballing me, inmate? Don't be eyeballing me, inmate!" I was thinking, "No, I don't want to look into your eyes, CO." Then they walked me to a room where I was instructed to strip naked and shower with a bunch of other women. (Fortunately I had been working out so it wasn't as embarrassing as it could have been, you know, after bearing four children and nursing three.) No shower curtains just showerheads—get in, wash, get out. I put on my uniform and remained alert for further instructions. Then we marched (oh yeah, I forgot to mention we marched everywhere we went) to another building and waited to be instructed. In this building we (about 150 to two hundred women) waited for instructions.

This big woman, who looked to me like she was about six feet two and a solid 295 pounds, nicknamed me "Scary." She kept making comments and jokes about my new nickname and started pulling other people in on the joke. At first it made me mad because I didn't want people to see that I really was terrified; I was doing my damnedest to conceal it and look, as well as actually act, fearless. For one, I knew fear was a tool of the enemy, but here she would do things such as, if I dropped my pencil, she would say, "Scary, you dropped your pencil" or "Scary, you have to do this or that like this." I started to realize that she was trying to help me, and the joke about me being scary actually helped me, because after a while, even I had to laugh (a little bit). I saw that as big as she was, she wasn't my enemy; she was trying to help me on the "DL" (down low). At first I kept thinking, "You in the big house now with professional criminals. This isn't the county jail; you're with the real McCoy now." However, they were not all monsters (like me, for instance), and even the ones who were monsters probably weren't thinking about me because they didn't know what relation the big girl was to me. (Yes, I was just talking to myself to keep my sanity in case you were wondering.) See, in prison if someone claims you and somebody else tries to mess with you, that's a fight. I'm not saying that she claimed me, but people didn't know, and "big girl" was not the type that you would want to take a chance with. In the end she turned out to be a gentle giant who knew the word (Bible) and suffered from diabetes and seizures. Actually the prison wasn't giving her the proper medication, and this was causing her to have violent seizures. She would hurt herself falling on those concrete floors. I felt so bad for her. One time she volunteered to sing in the church service. She sang "I Won't Complain," and she could *sing*; it brought tears to my eyes. I never knew what she was in there for, but she had some good in her.

Prison Fight!

After around six weeks in diagnostics, I was shipped off to the prison where I was going to be housed. When I first got there, on my way to the chow hall, I saw a girl who stood out. Maybe that's because she was smiling at me, but she didn't appear to have the same dark cloud over her that most of the women seemed to be carrying with them. However, I didn't pay her any mind as I continued on to the chow hall for lunch. If I remember correctly, you only got about ten to fifteen minutes to eat, and that was fine with me because I had no intention of eating that food. When lunch was over, as we were marching back to the dorm, I saw that girl again. She had a pleasant look about her, almost a glow. Fair skinned and around my height, with glasses and shoulder-length twists in her hair, she spoke and I spoke back. Later on it was time for yard call. I didn't want to go, but I didn't have a choice. I grabbed my Walkman and one of my Kenneth Copeland books and walked around the circumference of the yard. Then I noticed someone walking with me. It was that girl. She said her name was Kim and asked what mine was. I told her and she said, "I think I saw you on the news. You was out there in Putnam County, right?" I didn't say anything, and she said, "Oh, I'm familiar with your case. I live close by there."

I had been warned by a member of the staff when I first got there not to discuss any of my business with anyone because of my charges. Since it was on the news, everyone probably already knew everything if they watched TV, and while I was there, most people did. The inmates would know who committed what crime, and they would be expecting them. Surprisingly, a lot of people were familiar with the organization and its doctrine and were in support of it. If your case made it to the news, depending on what it was and how the majority felt about it, they treated you like a celebrity. She noticed my book and asked what I was reading. I showed her the title, and she said she read his books too. So we talked about the word for a while. Then out of the blue she said, "If anybody asks about your charges, just tell them armed robbery, and if they have any more questions, they can ask me. I'll be your body guard." She had some connections (back up).

We became friends and no one ever questioned me, but everyone knew Kim. We were always together so I guess people assumed she had claimed me, and I didn't care if it meant people weren't going to mess with me. A few months went by, and I requested to in the faith-based dorm where the focus was on the various sects of religion. It was a peaceful dorm. Kim moved there also, but we stayed on different halls. One day Kim must have fallen and bumped her head because I was talking with a few of the girls in our hall while waiting for them to call count. (Every certain amount of hours the prison would lock everyone down so it could count all the inmates and make sure we were all there.) One of the girls on the hall was Kim's nemesis, so when Kim saw her talking with me, she went ballistic. Kim grabbed my arm and pushed me to my cell, yelling, "Go to your cell; don't talk to her." I pulled away from her and said, "Get the hell off of me! You must be crazy." She was pulling on me, I was pushing her off, and we tripped and fell to the ground.

A few people pulled us apart, and then the officer had us taken to the hole. This was crazy to me, but if you are attacked in prison, you're not supposed to fight back. So according to the officer on duty and witnesses, she attacked me and I didn't fight her, so after about an hour in the hole, they let me out. Kim stayed in there for a few days or so. On the way to the hole, officers and inmates alike were saying, "Noooo, not Candace, she don't bother nobody, but Kim on the other hand has been in several fights." It felt kind of good to hear people supporting me because I didn't know if "Kim's people" were gonna come after me just for GP - *general purposes*." Thank God they didn't, and Kim ended up apologizing to me. Glad it didn't turn out like those prison fights in the movies, whew! But, you know, one thing by the grace of God I was not afraid to fight her—maybe because she was my size.

The Shower Scene

All I have to say about that is *don't drop the soap*!

Chapter 9
May 8th

From my daughter's perspective

My mom asked me what happened on May 8, 2002, and how it has affected my life. My name is Brandi, and at the time of the arrest, I was nine years old going on ten. It was a hot and sunny day, and the sky was bright blue with scattered, fluffy white clouds. The air was always so fresh and crisp, and a slight breeze topped off what seemed to be such a perfect summer day. School had just let out for the summer break. I remember running down the hill to one hundred (a ranch-style house), which was the number given to the house in which I resided. I was looking for my mom because progress reports were in, and I was excited to show her my grades. I was told that she, my dad, and a few others had left the land to go to a store. So I decided to take off my school uniform and put on my play clothes. I made a pack of ramen noodles and walked to the tennis court. There was a really big oak tree right beside the court, and I sat under it while I ate my noodles. A few of my friends were on the playground, so I dropped my dishes off at the house and made my way to the playground. There was this wooden jungle gym that we would hang out under because of the shade.

We had just gotten comfortable when we spotted a

helicopter. As kids, we weren't exposed too much to things "out in the world," as we would call it, so we were intrigued by the sight of the helicopter so close to the ground. We saw one of the brothers running toward us yelling, "Go in the house!" We were wondering why and decided to ignore him. He shouted again for us to go to the house, so we all ran down to one hundred. I was kind of happy because my friends were with me. We went toward the den, stopping by a nearby room across the hall to see who was there. We then made our way to the den where a few of the other children were, including my little brother Bobby and my youngest sibling. We found a movie to watch, but before we could press "play," we were interrupted by a very loud *bang* at the door. Natural instinct sent us running for cover. I was under my bed with my little brother and one of my friends. We were so frightened and completely unaware of what was to come. After a second *bang* and a third *bang*, which was the loudest, we heard the double wooden door flying open and a loud deep voice yelling, "Come out with your hands in the air!" So we came out of hiding with our hands in the air. I remember feeling my heart drop into my stomach and thinking this was it. They made us form a line. There were about five really tall men dressed in full SWAT gear with big assault rifles, maybe M16s, aimed at all of our backs. They directed us toward the living room where the rest of the people were and told us to sit down while they looked around. The grandmother of the house began to sing Sunday school songs to try and comfort the crying children. I remember wishing I was with my mom.

THE MAIN WIFE

The men returned and told us that they had arrested my
mother, father, and few others. I felt as if I had just got
socked in the stomach and began crying profusely, wondering why. Everyone gasped with disbelief and began crying.
The officers said they'd explain more at a later time. One
of the officers removed his head gear to wipe his sweat and
told us he was only doing his job.

We were later escorted to the temple where we would
have Sunday school. Everyone was there seated, and the
officers explained that my mother, my father, and a few
others were arrested in front of a store in Milledgeville,
a nearby town. They would remain in their custody until
further notice. They began calling out the names of a few
of the teen boys and girls, five to be exact. Four girls, two
of them twins, were about sixteen years old, and the other
two were between fourteen and sixteen. The youngest was
my older brother, John, who was then thirteen years old.
When they first began calling out names, no one said anything. When they called my brother John's name, a woman
stood up and said, "He's here sitting by me." Everyone kind
of looked at her in disbelief, almost as if she had betrayed
us. I waited for hours for my brother to return. We were
always so close; whenever I cried, he'd cry and vice versa. I
was his baby sister. He never returned, so I started asking
if anyone had seen him. One of the young girls around my
age told me they took him and the other four girls in a van.
My heart sank once again, and I couldn't conceal my tears.
I felt as if the life had been sucked out of me.

We sat in the temple for hours, conversing among

ourselves, trying to understand what was going on. They handed out packaged lunches in brown paper bags, some hoagies, some peanut butter and jelly sandwiches. We were told by the adults with us not to eat the hoagies because they were pork—not that we were Muslim anymore; it was just one of the things that stuck with us throughout the years of constant change of religion. One by one the officers started calling out names, taking each one of us into a room connected to the room we were all in. There was an opening, almost like a big window, that allowed the people in the temple to see what was going on. They were fingerprinting everyone; taking photos while they held signs with numbers on them, almost like prisoners; and taking down birthdates and the names of the parents. Then they put a yellow wristband on their arms. As the night went on, the amount of people began to dwindle to very few; once they received wristbands they were told to exit the premises. My little brother and I were the only two who hadn't been fingerprinted or given a wristband. They called out for the remaining people, which were just me and my little brother. They were notified that our mom was the one who had been arrested earlier that day, so the officer for Dfacs came toward us, and my aunt on my dad's side decided to take us. We went back to one hundred to gather our things, and the house was a wreck. Clothes, toys, and furniture were thrown everywhere. We gathered what we could and headed toward Atlanta, Georgia.

About six of us were at my aunt's, and we all slept on the floor in the hallway that night until we were able to settle in and divide into rooms. I don't even remember my birthday that year. Time had gone by, and the company of a few of my siblings had eased the pain. One day we were all watching the television and happened to flip to the news channel. We spotted our dad in an orange jumpsuit with chains on his hands and feet; his head was hung low in shame. Reality overshadowed our happiness as we suddenly remembered why we were where we were. We'd never seen him look that way. He was always well dressed and walked proudly. The things they were saying about him were horrible things we thought only a monster could do. It had been six months, and there still had been no word from or about my mom. That really bothered me, but the following day my aunt said my brother and I could go see our mother. We were so excited and couldn't wait until that weekend to see her.

The first visit was hard because she was behind thick glass, and we had to talk to her on a phone. She had the orange jumpsuit on as well, and though it broke our hearts to see her that way, we were still excited to see our mother. The hardest part was watching her leave and knowing that she wasn't coming home with us. As time went on we got used to the visits, but they were always bittersweet.

All of the children at my aunt's house had gone on to live with their parents or other family members, so only my little brother and I remained. People were also living on the land once again and continuing on with their lives. Although a lot of our siblings had returned, they had at least one parent present. We didn't, so we stayed with our aunt. Occasionally we would spend time up there during events and what not. Eventually my aunt got sick of the responsibility and called my grandfather to come and get us. From there, life as we knew it changed. We loved staying with our grandfather and going with him to visit our mom. Time had passed, and my mom was able to post bail. We were all so happy with this news and couldn't wait for her to arrive. The day she came home we were on the land and had to drive out to Covington, Georgia, where my grandfather lived. We were anxious; it had been a long ride, but we finally arrived. My heart was pounding when we walked in, and there she was. She didn't seem as excited as we thought she would be, but we still embraced and sat and talked with her. She looked great, and we knew she was happy to be with her family and eat normal food again.

The time came for school to start, and she enrolled us in public school for the first time. I was in sixth grade, and my little brother was in fourth grade. I was always awkward and antisocial, but through the whole ordeal it had gotten worse. I was so nervous to go to school for the first day. I remember she woke us up that morning with breakfast ready, and she walked us down to the school bus. We were too afraid the first time, and my grandfather ended up driving us to school the first week. All the kids were so much different than I was used to. They had permed hair and wore shorts and miniskirts. I had these two puffs in my hair, and I wore this beige jumper and Skechers sneakers. I thought I looked OK, but the other children didn't think so. They would make fun of my hair, my clothes, and the way I talked. I hated going to school and riding the bus. I didn't make many friends in the beginning and usually stayed to myself. I talked to my mom about what was going on at school and asked her if she could perm my hair too. She told me I didn't need that, but if that's what I wanted, OK. So we got a kiddie perm and did it—not that it changed my hair much—but I felt a little more comfortable, like I was blending in with the rest of the girls.

Time passed and we had friends and enjoyed school. My mom still woke us up every morning, reciting the Lord's Prayer, and had breakfast ready. We loved that. She had even made a friend in the neighborhood. We would go to visit my older brother John who was in foster care in Eatonton, Georgia. We missed him so much, and visiting him was always so much fun. He'd always have plenty of candy for me and my little brother. My granddad would pick up Subway sandwiches, and we'd sit in this visiting room where we would eat and talk and laugh. My mom wasn't able to see him yet, but he'd sneak a peek or wave at her here and there from the car. One day we found out that Mommy had to go to court for sentencing and wouldn't be coming back home that day. We were devastated and dreaded the moment we had to say our good-byes. The day had come, and I remember watching her get ready to go. She put on a sweat suit and removed all of her jewelry because she said she wouldn't need it. I admired her at that moment. She was so strong, and although her face was swollen from crying, not once had I seen a tear. She remained so strong in front of us. My little brother and I kept our composure until the moment she left. We hugged her good-bye, and they went on their way. It was a gloomy morning, and the overcast seemed to match our moods. The first time kind of prepared us for this, so we went outside with our friends and being with them eased the pain. We started visiting our mom every weekend, but this time it was contact visits. Contact visits mean that we didn't have to see her from behind a glass. That was amazing, and just something as simple as a hug from her every weekend made the journey that much easier. Later that year, my grandfather was granted custody of my older brother, and he finally was able to come and live with us.

In Closing

God has given me peace through his word, and now whenever I go through a storm, I can always look back and reflect on how God came through for me time and time again. Through my ups and downs, I was able to find myself and my inner strength. Know that I am revealing my life's events to help another and give hope to those who cannot see the light at the end of the tunnel. Tomorrow is always better than today. I was on a different path in the beginning, not knowing what lay ahead. I can honestly thank him for all my trials and tribulations as well as my triumphs. They made me strong and confident in myself and my relationship with God.

Thank you, Lord. Thank you, Jesus!

CPSIA information can be obtained at www.ICGtesting.com
Printed in the USA
LVOW07s0428301014

411049LV00001B/211/P

9 781478 730194